Fire Safety

by Lisa M. Herrington

Content Consultant

Debra Holtzman, J.D., M.A.

Reading Consultant

Jeanne Clidas, Ph.D.
Reading Specialist

Children's Press®
An Imprint of Scholastic Inc.
New York Toronto London Auckland Sydney
Mexico City New Delhi Hong Kong
Danbury, Connecticut

Dear Parent/Educator:
It is very important that children learn fire safety rules. However, this is something they might need help with from a grown-up. If your child needs that help, we hope you will use this book as a springboard to a discussion about fire safety with him or her. You can read the book together the first time, and talk about the different suggestions inside.

Library of Congress Cataloging-in-Publication Data
Herrington, Lisa M.
  Fire safety / by Lisa M. Herrington.
    p. cm. — (Rookie read-about safety)
  Includes index.
  Audience: Ages 3-6
  ISBN 978-0-531-28970-9 (library binding) ISBN 978-0-531-29272-3 (pbk.)
  1. Fire prevention—Juvenile literature. I. Title.
TH9148.H47 2012
363.377—dc23   2012013375

Produced by Spooky Cheetah Press

2 3 4 5 6 7 8 9 10 R 22 21 20 19 18 17 16 15 14 13

Photographs © 2013: Alamy Images/Nancy Greifenhagen, Nancy G Fire Photography: 15; Corbis Images/Richard T. Nowitz: 24; Getty Images/David McNew: 20; iStockphoto: 16 (Lorraine Boogich), 12 (slobo); James Levin Studios: cover photograph, 23 foreground; Kevin P. Hannafin, community educator, retired F.D.N.Y., (1982-2003), HOOPER THE FIREHOUSE DOG "sm" (1990-1999), E-211/L-119, Brooklyn, N.Y.: cover; Masterfile/Philip Rostron: 28; Richard Hutchings Photography: 27; Shutterstock, Inc.: 3 (Anita Patterson Peppers), 19 (Losevsky Pavel), 8 (Milan Vasicek); Thinkstock: 31 top left (Hemera), 7, 11, 23 background, 31 bottom right, 31 bottom left (iStockphoto), 31 top right (Jupiterimages, Creatas Images), 4 (Jupiterimages/Getty Images).

Table of Contents

Be Fire Safe

Being safe around
fire is important.
Learn fire safety rules!

Always ask a grown-up
for help in the kitchen.
Stay away from stoves,
microwaves, and toasters.

Do not ever touch candles, matches, or lighters. Those are for grown-up use!

Only grown-ups should use the fireplace. Stay away! Do not ever touch the fireplace, even after the fire has gone out.

Be Ready!

Your home should have smoke alarms. You will hear a loud noise if they sense smoke. A grown-up should test the batteries and change them twice a year.

Make a fire escape plan with your family. Plan at least two safe ways out of each room.

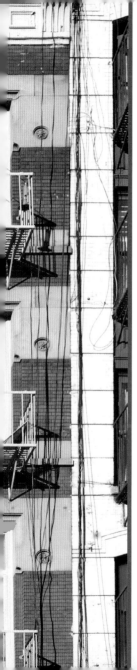

Remember never to use an elevator during a fire. You can get trapped. Plan to use the stairs or a fire escape.

Choose a safe place to meet outside your home. Practice your plan!

DO NOT CROSS

Get Out and Stay Out!

If there is a fire, get out and stay out. Go to your meeting place.

Before opening a door, feel it.
If the door is hot, do not open it.
Find another way out. Leave
everything behind.

Is there smoke? Stay low and get out of the house. Smoke rises in a fire. The safest air is low.

If your clothes are on fire, do not run. Stop, drop, and roll. Cover your face with your hands.

stop

drop

roll

27

28

Do not hide from firefighters. They are there to help. Call out so they can find you. That is how you will be fire safe!

Try It! Go back to page 26 and read the safety tip. Now you try it—stop, drop, and roll! Can you recall three other fire safety tips?

I Can Be Safe!

- Check smoke alarms. Replace the batteries twice a year.

- With your family, make a fire-escape plan. Practice the plan often.

- If a fire starts, get out and stay out. Stay out no matter what!

- Stop, drop, and roll if your clothes catch fire.

Words You Know

fire

firefighter

smoke alarm

toaster

Index

Facts for Now

Visit this Scholastic Web site for more information on fire safety:
www.factsfornow.scholastic.com
Enter the keyword **Fire**

About the Author

Lisa M. Herrington writes print and digital materials for kids, teachers, and parents. She lives in Connecticut with her husband and daughter. She hopes all kids stay safe!